GARBAGE GORGERS
OF THE ANIMAL WORLD

by Jody Sullivan Rake

Content Consultant:
David Stephens, PhD
Professor of Ecology, Evolution, and Behavior
University of Minnesota

Reading Consultant:
Barbara J. Fox
Professor Emerita
North Carolina State University

CAPSTONE PRESS
a capstone imprint

Blazers is published by Capstone Press,
1710 Roe Crest Drive, North Mankato, Minnesota 56003
www.capstonepub.com

Library of Congress Cataloging-in-Publication Data
Rake, Jody Sullivan, author.
 Garbage gorgers of the animal world / By Jody Sullivan Rake.
   pages cm. — (Blazers. Disgusting creature diets)
 Summary: "Discusses various organisms throughout the world that consume garbage as a part of their diets"—Provided by publisher.
 Includes bibliographical references and index.
ISBN 978-1-4914-1999-1 (library binding)
ISBN 978-1-4914-2176-5 (eBook PDF)
1. Scavengers (Zoology)—Juvenile literature. 2. Animals—Food—Juvenile literature. 3. Animal behavior—Juvenile literature. I. Title.
 QL756.5.R35 2015
 591.5—dc23
                         2014029720

Editorial Credits
Abby Colich, editor; Kyle Grenz, designer; Jo Miller, media researcher; Katy LaVigne, production specialist

Photo Credits
Alamy: FLPA, 18-19, Pep Roig, 28; Dreamstime: Lim Liang Jin, 14-15; Glow Images: All Canada Photos/ Bob Gurr, 13, First Light/Thomas Kitchin & Victoria Hurst, 10, Stocktrek Images/Terry Moore, 20-21; Newscom: Minden Pictures/Michael Durham, 6, 8-9; Robert Harding: Okapia/Ingo Arndt, 22-23; Science Source: Nigel Cattlin, 24-25, Tom McHugh, cover; Shutterstock: Sebastian Kaulitzki, 26-27; SuperStock: Biosphoto, 16-17, NaturePL, 4-5

Printed in China by Nordica.
1014/CA21401515
092014   008470NORDS15

TABLE OF CONTENTS

TALKING TRASH

All animals eat to survive. Some animal **diets** are weird. Others are just plain gross! Garbage is a part of many animal diets. These animals have **adapted** to eat the trash that humans throw away.

diet—what an animal eats
adapt—to change to fit into a new or different environment

4

gull

HUNGRY RATS

Brown rats are the most common garbage eaters. These rats live anywhere that humans live. Brown rats eat almost anything, but they have a balanced diet. They search through garbage cans for meat, grains, nuts, and fruit.

Fact!
While rats are not picky eaters, they do not like stale or spoiled food.

MASKED BANDITS

In most of North America, raccoons tear through trash at night. These masked **mammals** eat almost anything. Raccoons lift trash can lids with their long fingers. They search trash cans for leftover food.

Fact!

Raccoons aren't choosy, but they are clean. Before eating they often wash their food in whatever water they can find.

mammal—an animal with hair or fur that gives birth to young and feeds them milk

THUMBED OPOSSUMS

Opossums look like big rats. They are the only **marsupials** in North America. Opossums carry their young in pouches. They have another special body part—thumbs! Thumbs make it easier to sort through trash.

Fact!

Opossums compete with rats and cockroaches for food. Sometimes rats and cockroaches are their food!

marsupial—a mammal that carries its young in a pouch

THE BEAR FACTS

Bears usually eat plants and small animals. They are also garbage eaters. Bears help themselves to food in trash cans. If humans have food nearby, bears will find it. These big animals need to eat lots of food.

Fact!

Bears have a strong sense of smell. Bears use their good sense of smell to lead them to food and trash.

GARBAGE-EATING GOATS

Goats are adventurous eaters. They nose around trash looking for scraps of food. These curious creatures chew on anything that looks tasty. Paper, cardboard, and fabric are some of their favorite things to chew.

Fact!
Many people drink goat milk
and eat goat cheese.

Fact!
Gulls normally live near the water. But sometimes they are seen around trash dumps hundreds of miles from the water.

WHAT A GULL WANTS

If you have been near a large lake or ocean, you've probably seen gulls. To these birds nearly anything is a snack. Gulls near the sea eat **tide pool** creatures, dead sea animals, and human trash. Don't leave your beach picnic unguarded. They'll eat your meal too!

tide pool—a small pool that forms at low tide on rocky beaches

AS THE CROW FLIES

Crows are found all over the world. How did these black birds become so widespread? By being smart eaters. They know where to find a good meal, even in a nearby garbage can.

Fact!

Crows are smart birds. Scientists have watched them use tools to reach food.

Fact!

Tiger sharks are the least picky eaters of all sharks. They eat sea creatures that other sharks won't eat.

GARBAGE CANS OF THE SEA

Tiger sharks have been found with enough garbage in their stomachs to fill a Dumpster. Bottles, license plates, and even a chicken coop have been found in their stomachs. That's why these sharks are nicknamed "garbage cans of the sea."

GIANT GARBAGE EATERS

Coconut crabs live on islands in the Indian Ocean. These giant creatures usually eat fruit and coconuts. But they also love eating leftovers they find in trash cans.

RUBBISH FOR ROACHES

Cockroaches enjoy a good diet anywhere humans live. They are often only active at night. Garbage cans are perfect homes for them. Cockroaches nibble bits of food stuck to the trash.

HOORAY FOR BACTERIA!

Bacteria are tiny **organisms** that live everywhere. Some bacteria make you sick. Some bacteria keep you healthy. Bacteria break down food in the garbage that animals have not eaten.

organism—a living thing

bacteria

Fact!
The waste from billions of bacteria is what makes garbage smell so bad.

DEADLY DIET

Sometimes eating trash is harmful to animals. Animals eat many things in the trash that aren't good for them, such as plastic. Eating plastic can make animals sick or even kill them. Always throw away trash properly.

Fact!

The best practice for preventing deadly animal diets is to reduce, reuse, and recycle!

GLOSSARY

adapt (uh-DAPT)—to change to fit into a new or different environment

diet (DY-uht)—what an animal eats

mammal (MAM-uhl)—an animal with hair or fur that gives birth to young and feeds them milk

marsupial (mar-SOO-pee-uhl)—a mammal that carries its young in a pouch

organism (OR-guh-niz-uhm)—a living thing

tide pool (TYD POOL)—a small pool that forms at low tide on rocky beaches

READ MORE

Berne, Emma Carlson. *Opossums*. Scavengers: Eating Nature's Trash. New York: PowerKids Press, 2014.

Bodden, Valerie. *Cockroaches*. Creepy Creatures. Mankato, Minn.: Creative Education, 2013.

Jordens, Rob. *Scavengers of the Animal Kingdom*. St. Johnsbury, Ver.: Compass Publishing, 2013.

INTERNET SITES

FactHound offers a safe, fun way to find Internet sites related to this book. All of the sites on FactHound have been researched by our staff.

Here's all you do:

Visit *www.facthound.com*

Type in this code: 9781491419991

Super-cool stuff!

Check out projects, games and lots more at
www.capstonekids.com

INDEX